Daily *warm-ups*

POETRY

J. WESTON
WALCH
PUBLISHER
Portland, Maine

D1417246

Shari Goldberg

Permissions Editor
J. Weston Walch, Publisher
321 Valley Street • P.O. Box 658
Portland, Maine 04104-0658

1   2   3   4   5   6   7   8   9   10
ISBN 0-8251-4520-1

Copyright © 2003
J. Weston Walch, Publisher
P.O. Box 658 • Portland, Maine 04104-0658
www.walch.com
Printed in the United States of America

The **Daily Warm-Ups series** is a wonderful way to turn extra classroom minutes into valuable learning time. The 180 quick activities—one for each day of the school year—review, practice, and teach poetry skills. These daily activities may be used at the very beginning of class to get students into learning mode, near the end of class to make good educational use of that transitional time, in the middle of class to shift gears between lessons—or whenever else you have minutes that now go unused. In addition to providing students with structure and focus, they are a natural path to other classroom activities involving writing and vocabulary skills. As students build their vocabularies and become more adept at word analysis, they will be better prepared for standardized tests, such as the PSAT and SAT.

Daily Warm-Ups are easy-to-use reproducibles—simply photocopy the day's activity and distribute it. Or make a transparency of the activity and project it on the board. You may want to use the activities for extra credit points or as a check on the vocabulary development skills that are built and acquired over time.

However you choose to use them, *Daily Warm-Ups* are a convenient and useful supplement to your regular lesson plans. Make every minute of your class time count!

Freely write your answers to the following questions.

- How would you define the word poem?

- What kinds of words are in poems?

- What do poems sound like?

- How is a poem like a song?

- How can it be like a story?

- Have you ever written a poem?

- Would you like to?

1

Think of a word

and write it in the middle of the page. Draw a circle around it. Now draw some spokes out of the circle. On each spoke, write a new word that the first word makes you think of. Next, circle each new word and draw some spokes out of it. What does each new word make you think of? Keep going with new words and spokes until the whole page is filled. Are all of the words you wrote connected in some way? Can you think of ways to connect the ones that are very different from each other?

Daily Warm-Ups: Poetry

2

William Shakespeare writes a witch's spell in the form of a poem in his play *Macbeth*. The witches get together over their cauldron, or boiling pot, and call for ingredients:

Double, double, toil and trouble;
Fire burn, and cauldron bubble.
Fillet of a fenny snake,
In the cauldron boil and bake;
Eye of newt and toe of frog,
Wool of bat and tongue of dog,

Adder's fork and blind-worm's
   sting,
Lizard's leg and howlet's wing,
For a charm of pow'rful trouble,
Like a hell-broth boil and bubble.

Write a poem from the voice of a witch or wizard about weird and grotesque things that you need to cast a spell. You may want to say what the spell will do or whom it is for. You can rhyme it, as Shakespeare did, if you like. Here is an example:

To make the trees bow down to me
I need items from the ends of the earth
Heart of moth and head of fly
A whole beetle, which first must die . . .

Write a poem that is a "want ad" looking for someone to take on a responsibility you are sick of having. Try to include why you no longer want the job, how the job will need to be done, and its benefits, if any. For example:

Wanted

Someone to brush my teeth at night
Must have steady hand
Good at squeezing toothpaste without getting it all over the sink
Must know when I need a new toothbrush
Must never get so tired, like I do,
     that you just say "forget it" and climb into bed until Mom yells.
      If you are good, the dentist will give you a sticker instead of a filling.

4

Daily Warm-Ups: Poetry

An *acrostic* is a poem in which the first letter of every line spells out a word when read going down. Usually, the poem is about the word, like this:

> **C**an you imagine the speed?
> **A**venue after avenue,
> **R**acing to get there first.

Write your name or favorite word going down the page. Now write an acrostic about you or about that word.

5

You can also write an acrostic with your name or a word going up the page:

> So many lights
> Riding the night
> A shooting brightness
> Traces a pattern
> Sings to the sky

Write your name or favorite word going up the page. Write an acrostic about you or about the word.

6

Read the first stanza of "Spring" by Gerard Manley Hopkins, aloud if possible:

Nothing is so beautiful as Spring—
When weeds, in wheels, shoot long and lovely and lush;
Thrush's eggs look little low heavens, and thrush
Through the echoing timber does so rinse and wring
The ear, it strikes like lightnings to hear him sing;
The glassy peartree leaves and blooms, they brush
The descending blue; that blue is all in a rush
With richness; the racing lambs too have fair their fling.

Hopkins's language is very full and rich, filled with lots of expressive words and sounds that seem to tumble into each other. Choose a topic that seems very exciting and full of life to you and write a poem about it. Try to write in an overflowing kind of style, as Hopkins did.

7

Write the opposite of each word below. They're words that don't usually have opposites, so be creative with your answers.

Singing

Crash

Writing

Wall

Daily Warm-Ups: Poetry

8

Ben Jonson wrote a poem called "Inviting a Friend to Supper." Here is part of it:

> Tonight, grave Sir, both my poor house and I
> > Do equally desire your company:
> Not that we think us worthy such a guest . . .
> Yet shall you have, to rectify your palate,
> > An olive, capers, or some better salad,
> Ushering the mutton; with a short-legged hen,
> > If we can get her, full of eggs, and then
> Lemons, and wine for sauce . . .

Jonson doesn't feel worthy of his friend's company, but he invites him anyway and tries to entice him with delicious dishes. Think of someone famous you'd like to invite to your house, and write a poem asking him or her to a wonderful meal. You can make it sound like a fancy invitation, if you want: "Tonight, Queen Elizabeth, I desire your company . . . You shall eat pizza with me, and lemonade . . ." You can also write about what the conversation will be like and who else (if anyone) will be coming.

9

Onomatopoeia is a very long word for a pretty simple thing. It is when a word sounds like what it means. "Buzz" sounds like an insect flying by your ear; "meow" sounds like a cat asking for dinner. Thomas Nashe wrote a poem about spring in which he made up words to sound like bird calls: "jug-jug, pu-we, to-witta-woo!" Write some animal words that are onomatopoeic. Then see if you can write a whole line that sounds like it is coming from one animal; for example: "Roar! Grrrr! Wraeow!" for a lion.

Daily Warm-Ups: Poetry

10

Every poem has a *speaker*. The speaker is the person or animal or being that we imagine speaking the poem. It may be the writer of the poem, but it doesn't have to be. Could you write a poem from someone else's perspective, or as if it is being spoken by a made-up character?

Write a poem in which you are the speaker, talking about something that happened to you yesterday. Then write it again, from another perspective, with a different speaker. For example, if the first poem is about how you argued with a bus driver, the second poem's speaker might be the bus driver or another passenger on the bus.

11

A **dramatic monologue** is a kind of poem in which we hear a character in the middle of a story. The character is not the poet, but someone else, and the entire poem is spoken by that character. Usually, the poem begins at a crazy moment in the story, and we aren't quite sure what is going on. As the character continues speaking, however, we learn about the situation. For example, read this excerpt from the beginning of Robert Browning's poem "Mr. Sludge, 'The Medium.'" Who do you think is speaking the poem? What is going on?

> Now, don't sir! Don't expose me! Just this once!
> That was the first and only time, I'll swear,—
> Look at me, see, I kneel,—the only time,
> I swear, I ever cheated, . . .
>   Go tell them! Who the devil cares
> What such a rowdy chooses to . . .
>   Aie-aie-aie!
> Please, sir! Your thumbs are through my windpipe, sir!
> Ch-ch!

Can you imagine what happens next in the story? Write another five lines to follow the ones here. Remember to stay in the voice of the character speaking.

12

Fill in the following blanks with answers that aren't true but that you like to imagine. Make them as detailed or complicated as you like.

I eat _____ for breakfast.

I carry _____ in my backpack.

Every afternoon I make a trip to _____.

My best friend is _____.

I never go anywhere without _____.

I go swimming in _____.

I have _____ in my room at home.

Yesterday, someone called and offered me _____.

There is a _____ hiding in my locker.

13

Write a poem about some kind of skin—something that covers, encloses, or protects something else. Try to be imaginative; what about the skins of buildings or furniture? You could also think about human skin in an imaginative way: do people put on different types of skin for different occasions? How is your school skin different from your party skin? What parts of your skin won't ever change? How does an object look without its skin?

14

In this poem called "The Poplar-Field," William Cowper writes about poplar trees that he played in growing up; they have since been plowed away:

> The poplars are felled, farewell to the shade
> And the whispering sound of the cool colonnade,
> The winds play no longer, and sing in the leaves,
> Nor Ouse on his bosom their image receives.
>
> Twelve years have elapsed since I last took a view
> Of my favourite field and the bank where they grew,
> And now in the grass behold they are laid,
> And the tree is my seat that once lent me a shade.

Write a poem about something you loved when you were younger that you no longer have. Write about what, if anything, has taken its place.

15

Robert Burns wrote this poem about his love called "A Red, Red Rose":

My love is like a red, red rose
   That's newly sprung in June:
My love is like the melody
   That's sweetly played in tune.

As fair art thou, my bonnie lass,
   So deep in love am I:
And I will love thee still, my dear,
   Till a' the seas gang dry. . . .

Burns uses the word "like" to compare his beautiful love to a fresh rose that's come up in June and to a sweet melody. Then he uses the word "as" to say that as fair (pretty) as his love is, that's how deeply in love he is—we understand that his love is very fair and he is very deeply in love. A *simile* is a comparison of two basically unlike things, using "like" or "as." Burns's love isn't really like a rose—she's not red or thorny or growing out of the ground—but her beauty and youth make him think of a perfect new rose.

Write three similes in which you compare people you know to things that grow out of the ground—flowers, fruits, vegetables, and plants are all fair game. Try to think about different aspects of the growing things—an apple is shiny, a weed is irritating, and a carrot has a long neck.

Daily Warm-Ups: Poetry

16

Write a poem about how something moves. It could be something alive or mechanical. Try to use not only adverbs—slowly, powerfully—but comparisons. For example: the flag waved peacefully, as if it had never been worried about anything.

17

© 2003 J. Weston Walch, Publisher

In a poem called "God's Grandeur," Gerard Manley Hopkins writes that the grandeur "will flame out, like shining from shook foil." The image is bright and startling and easy to see in our minds' eyes. Think of something that is miraculous or amazing to you and describe it with a comparison that expresses the feeling of wonder, excitement, and magic it inspires.

18

Daily Warm-Ups: Poetry

Write a poem about something—a feeling, event, or place—that you once tried to explain to someone and couldn't. You can either write about the thing itself or about why you had trouble explaining it.

Onomatopoeia doesn't only refer to animal noises. For example, "chug-a-chug-a" is onomatopoeia for the noise a train makes. The rhythm of a poem can also be a kind of onomatopoeia, if it sounds like the thing it describes. In this poem, called "The Drum," by John Scott, the first two lines of the poem have the rhythm of a beating drum:

> I hate that drum's discordant sound,
> Parading round, and round, and round…

20

Try to write a line of onomatopoeia in which the words and the rhythm sound like the thing you are describing. For example, this line is clunky at the beginning, when the train is trying to pull out of the station, and fast and easy at the end, when it's gone: Chug-a-chug, heavy, jostling, trying to tug, almost, almost—and off we go! Choo! Choo!

Read the poem "The Sick Rose," by William Blake
("thou" means "you"):

O Rose, thou art sick!
The invisible worm
That flies in the night,
In the howling storm.

Has found out thy bed
Of crimson joy,
And his dark secret love
Does thy life destroy.

Blake is telling the rose something that he knows but imagines the rose doesn't: a worm is inside the rose and will soon kill it. Write a poem to an animal or plant in which you tell it something you know, but it doesn't. Write it short, like Blake's, as if you are delivering a secret short message. Here are some examples:

If I don't feed you tonight, fish, I might find you floating tomorrow . . . .
You don't know it, daisy, but there is a little girl behind me about to pick your head off . . . .

21

Blake wrote other poems to creatures; here is part of one called "The Tiger" in which he wonders how such a frightening being was created:

Tiger! Tiger! burning bright
In the forests of the night,
What immortal hand or eye
Could frame thy fearful symmetry?

In what distant deeps or skies
Burned the fire of thine eyes?
On what wings dare he aspire?
What the hand dare seize the fire?

And what shoulder, and what art,
Could twist the sinews of thy
    heart?
And when thy heart began to beat,
What dread hand? And what dread
    feet?

22

Write a poem addressed to an animal that you've always found scary or "fearful." Ask it questions about how it feels and where it has come from. You can ask about a particular thing you've always been curious about or wished you could touch; for example,

Lion, is it scratchy when that mane starts to grow out of your head?
Are you bigger than your mom?
Would it tickle if I touched you under the arm?

Read this poem by William Collins, "Ode to Evening."

Don't worry about understanding what is going on; just pay attention to what the words are like and how they sound. You might want to read it aloud.

For when thy folding star arising shows
His paly circlet, at his warning lamp
    The fragrant Hours, and elves
    Who slept in flowers the day,

And many a nymph who wreathes her brows with sedge,
And sheds the freshening dew, and, lovelier still,
    The Pensive Pleasures sweet,
    Prepare thy shadowy car.

Choose the word or phrase that you like best from the poem above. You don't have to know what the word means. Some interesting ones are *folding star, paly, circlet, sedge, shadowy car.* Write a few sentences or lines that explain what you like about your choice. Is it how it sounds or looks or what it makes you think of? Do you usually like words with those letters? If you could rename anything in the world with your word, what object would you pick?

23

Part of a poem by Sir John Davies, "In Praise of Dancing," *personifies* the ocean, or describes it as if it were a person. The ocean's waves are referred to as "his" waves, and each wave is said to kiss the shore:

> Sometimes his proud green waves in order set,
> One after other, flow unto the shore;
> Which when they have with many kisses wet,
> They ebb away in order, as before.

Personification gives us a specific image of something by relating it to human actions and thoughts. Can you imagine how the waves seem to kiss the shore before they ebb, or return to the sea? What other words, usually used to describe human actions, might describe the way that waves land on the shore?

24

Think of any body of water—a lake, river, ocean, pond or bathtub—and write a poem personifying how it interacts with something else—the land, the sky, children, fish, plants, birds, boats, or anything else. Concentrate on giving the water a human action that isn't usually associated with it; for example: "The river held our small boat like a knapsack on its back, letting us bounce as it ran to meet its friends."

Pick a color and write a poem that uses it five times. You can describe things that are that color or use the color to represent a feeling. Here's an example:

> The sky was lavender, kissing good night to the trees before it went to sleep.
> I closed my eyes and saw lavender.
> There was lavender in my brain, in my bones, I could smell it.
> I curled up like a lavender cloud.
> I wanted to be held by the lavender.

25

© 2003 J. Weston Walch, Publisher

Write a poem about an object that usually looks ugly, but has somehow been attractive to you. For example, a broken bicycle that is twisted in a graceful way, the rainbow sheen on an oil slick, or a desert-like sand pile in a construction site.

Daily Warm-Ups: Poetry

26

Write a poem about something that is always thought of as beautiful, but that you have seen in a different way. For example, your classmates' favorite movie star who you think resembles your dentist, or a car that looks like an ugly bug.

27

Daily Warm-Ups: Poetry

This is a whole poem of personification by Margaret Cavendish, Duchess of Newcastle. The poet imagines that melancholy—a sad, depressed feeling—is a woman, and each line of the poem describes her personality or the way she lives.

> Her voice is low and gives a hollow sound;
> She hates the light and is in darkness found
> Or sits with blinking lamps, or tapers small,
> Which various shadows make against the wall.
> She loves naught else but noise which discord makes;
> As croaking frogs whose dwelling is in lakes;
> The raven's hoarse, the mandrake's hollow groan
> And shrieking owls which fly i' the night alone;
> The tolling bell, which for the dead rings out;
> A mill, where rushing waters run about;
> The roaring winds, which shake the cedars tall,
> Plough up the seas, and beat the rocks withal.

28

Choose an emotion—maybe something complex, such as fear or anger or excitement—and write a poem in which you personify it. Think of the kinds of "personality traits" that Cavendish does: what noises does your emotion like? What kind of walks does it take? Where does it sleep?

In Shakespeare's Sonnet #130, he pokes fun at the usual ways for describing a woman's beauty:

My mistress' eyes are nothing like the sun;
Coral is far more red than her lips' red;
If snow be white, why then her breasts are dun;
If hair be wires, black wires grow on her head.
I have seen roses damask'd, red and white,
But no such roses see I in her cheeks,
And in some perfumes is there more delight
Than in the breath that from my mistress reeks.
I love to hear her speak, yet well I know
That music hath a far more pleasing sound;
I grant I never saw a goddess go,
My mistress when she walks treads on the ground.
    And yet, by heaven, I think my love as rare
    As any she belied with false compare.

29

Write a poem about someone in which you recognize what he or she is not—beautiful as a painting, smart as Einstein—and explain why you like him or her anyway.

Mary Matilda Betham wrote this poem to her friend Nancy, who decided she'd like to be called Anna:

Forgive me, if I wound your ear,
    By calling of you Nancy,
Which is the name of my sweet
    friend,
      The other's but her fancy.

Ah, dearest girl! how could your
    mind
      The strange distinction frame?

The whimsical, unjust caprice,
    Which robs you of your name.

Nancy agrees with what we see,
    A being wild and airy;
Gay as a nymph of Flora's train,
    Fantastic as a fairy.

30

The poet says that she won't call her friend Anna instead of Nancy because Nancy suits her better; it sounds "wild and airy" and "fantastic."

Have you ever wished for a different name, one which you think sounds more like you? Write a poem about a name you'd like to have and the feelings and characteristics you associate with it. You may want to contrast it to your own name. If you want to stick with your own name, write a poem about why it suits you.

Think of your favorite song. Rewrite the lyrics, keeping the rhythm. Try to form your lines so that they can still be sung with the music. You can choose to write about any subject you wish.

31

Lewis Carroll invented something called a *portmanteau word* in *Alice in Wonderland*. A portmanteau is a kind of suitcase, and Humpty Dumpty says that a portmanteau word has more than one meaning "packed up" into it. Humpty Dumpty explains the beginning of this poem, "Jabberwocky," to Alice:

> 'Twas brillig, and the slithy toves
> Did gyre and gimble in the wabe:
> All mimsy were the borogoves,
> And the mome raths outgrabe.

Humpty Dumpty says that "slithy" means lithe and slimy. Can you guess what the other portmanteau words in the poem mean? Write some of your own to describe what kind of day it is outside.

32

➤ *Goes with exercises 34 and 35*

Think of a short sentence that you heard someone say to you yesterday. A question would work well but you can use a statement, too; it should be about seven to ten words. For example, perhaps someone asked you, "But why do you keep repeating me?" Write the sentence down and make it all fit on one line. That's the first line of your poem. The rest of the poem can be about how the sentence made you feel or what you said (or wish you had said) in response.

33

Take the first line of your poem from yesterday and write it so that it takes up two lines. The line should "break"—the new one should start—at a point where the speaker might have paused. Keeping the same example as yesterday, this might be how you write it on two lines:

> But why
> do you keep repeating me?

Think about how breaking the line has altered the way it sounds or reads. Then use the two lines as the beginning of a new poem. How do the tone and feel of the poem change? Does it make you think of different things to write?

Daily Warm-Ups: Poetry

➤ *Goes with exercises 33 and 34*

Use the same line you started your poems with

yesterday and the day before. This time, write it on at least two lines—more if you wish—and try to make the breaks in places that aren't natural to the way the sentence was spoken. Here is an example:

> But why do
> you keep repeating
> me?

Again, write the rest of the poem and see how the new line breaks affect the way you write the poem. In the example, having "me" on a line all by itself might make you want to write about why you aren't repeating anyone else. Or, it might encourage you to make every line in the poem be three words or less.

35

Remember, a simile is a comparison of two normally unlike things using "like" or "as." Fill in the blanks to write the most imaginative similes you can think of—but be sure you can explain how the two things are similar. For example: "The blankets were wrinkled like <u>my uncle's face when he opens his mouth to speak</u>."

The shirt was as soft as _____.

I wanted to yell at him like _____.

She danced as if _____.

The coat felt like _____.

The noise got on my nerves like _____.

36

➤ *This is a group activity.*

Write down two first lines for poems. They can be about anything and sound like anything. For example, "I heard the clock tick and stopped," "The smooth hard loaf of bread on the table," "Creeping gently around the house."

Now, go around the classroom, each person reading his or her lines aloud. When you hear a line that you like, raise your hand to indicate that it's "yours." You cannot pick your own first line. When everyone has a first line, write the rest of your poem. It may be fun to read the poems aloud so that everyone can hear what has become of his or her first line.

37

Andrew Marvell describes being in a lush place in his poem "The Garden":

> What wondrous life is this I lead!
> Ripe apples drop about my head;
> The luscious clusters of the vine
> Upon my mouth do crush their wine;
> The nectarine and curious peach
> Into my hands themselves do reach;
> Stumbling on melons, as I pass,
> Ensnared with flowers, I fall on grass.

Daily Warm-Ups: Poetry

38

Write a poem about being in a beautiful, full garden. Like Marvell, talk about the things that you can eat, smell, see and touch. You can make the garden a little magical, the way that Marvell imagines the nectarine and peach reaching themselves into the speaker's hands.

Daily Warm-Ups: Poetry

James Weldon Johnson wrote these questions to "Black and unknown bards of long ago" ("bard" is another word for poet):

> How came your lips to touch the sacred fire?
> How, in your darkness, did you come to know
> The power and beauty of the minstrel's lyre?
> Who first from midst his bonds lifted his eyes?
> Who first from out the still watch, lone and long,
> Feeling the ancient faith of prophets rise
> Within his dark-kept soul, burst into song?

Think of a poem or poet that you admire. Write a poem that is all questions, asking the poet how she or he came to write such a beautiful thing. Draw on your own experience of writing poems to ask about the specific difficulties that the poet must have overcome; you could ask, How did you pay attention long enough to write all those lines? How did you come up with the first word? How did you know when to stop?

39

William Wordsworth wrote "Upon Westminster Bridge September 3, 1802" in London. Read the poem slowly and see if you can imagine the scene:

Earth has not anything to show more fair:
    Dull would he be of soul who could pass by
    A sight so touching in its majesty:
This City now doth, like a garment, wear
The beauty of the morning; silent, bare,
    Ships, towers, domes, theatres, and temples lie
    Open unto the fields, and to the sky;
All bright and glittering in the smokeless air.
Never did sun more beautifully steep
      In his first splendour, valley, rock, or hill;
    Ne'er saw I, never felt, a calm so deep!
      The river glideth at his own sweet will:
Dear God! the very houses seem asleep;
      And all that mighty heart is lying still!

Wordsworth describes the usually busy city before the workday has started, when it is "silent," "bright," and "calm." Write a poem about something that is usually very busy that you have seen in a calm state—maybe a city, supermarket, restaurant, or even a young child or puppy. Try to capture the moment of the quietness, as Wordsworth did. You may also want to write about how the experience affected you.

This poem called "Kubla Khan," by Samuel Taylor Coleridge, describes a fantastical made-up place:

> In Xanadu did Kubla Khan
> > A stately pleasure-dome decree:
>
> Where Alph, the sacred river, ran
> Through caverns measureless to man
> > Down to a sunless sea.
>
> So twice five miles of fertile ground
> With walls and towers were girdled round:
> And there were gardens bright with sinuous rills . . .
>
> The shadow of the dome of pleasure
> > Floated midway on the waves;
>
> Where was heard the mingled measure
> > From the fountain and the caves.
>
> It was a miracle of rare device,
> A sunny pleasure-dome with caves of ice!

First, underline all of the fantastic things about the pleasure-dome. Then try to imagine your own pleasure-dome—or a fantastic place with another shape or landscape. Write a poem describing it. You may want to include contrasting ideas (as in "A sunny pleasure-dome with caves of ice!").

41

© 2003 J. Weston Walch, Publisher

Repetition of one line throughout a poem can make the poem sound more musical—although it is a challenge to repeat a line and keep the poem interesting. Try to write a six-line poem in which at least three lines are the same, or almost the same. You can write about a journey. For example:

> The mountain up above me
> And my feet are nervous
> The mountain up above me
> I start the twisty climb
> The mountain up above me
> Soon it will be below me.

42

Get a dictionary or any textbook. Open it up and pick one word. Write it down. Do this five more times. Now, write a poem with all five words in it.

43

An abstract idea is a concept like love or friendship that you can feel and understand, but can't define absolutely. The objects and people that you associate with an abstract idea are usually personal, different from the associations someone else might have.

Write a poem that is a list of real objects that you associate with the abstract idea of home. You can include descriptions of the objects—"sparkling floor, even though there is grime around the burners"—but try to use objects, rather than explanations. You might want to start by freewriting about the objects that you see in your mind when you think of home; for example: dog bouncing to see you, bright yellow bathroom, backyard with crazy weeds everywhere. The poem can be called "Home."

44

In "Song," John Donne asks for things that are impossible:

> Go and catch a falling star
>> Get with child a mandrake root,
> Tell me where all past years are,
>> Or who cleft the Devil's foot;
> Teach me to hear mermaids singing
> Or to keep off envy's stinging . . . .

Write a poem in which you imagine you are sending someone on a quest to get or teach you things that seem impossible. You might want to know how to never get homework again, or why the wind whistles, or if the moon can visit your bedroom . . . anything. When you are finished making demands, let the person you asked answer and tell you whether or not you will get the things you ask for.

45

Read "The Land of Counterpane" by

Robert Louis Stevenson, which is about being home sick (a "counterpane" is a bedspread or quilt):

When I was sick and lay a-bed,
I had two pillows at my head,
And all my toys beside me lay
To keep me happy all the day.

And sometimes for an hour or so
I watched my leaden soldiers go,
With different uniforms and drills,
Among the bed-clothes, through
   the hills;

And sometimes sent my ships
   in fleets
All up and down among the
   sheets;
Or brought my trees and houses out,
And planted cities all about.

I was the giant great and still
That sits upon the pillow-hill,
And sets before him, dale and plain,
The pleasant land of counterpane.

46

Write a poem about what keeps you busy when you are sick and must stay in bed. If you watch TV or read books, you might want to write about the specific adventures you encounter, the way Stevenson writes about the land he invents.

John Skelton wrote short, abrupt lines that don't rhyme so well in order to make his poems funny. Here is an example, from his poem "Colin Clout," written in 1523:

> For though my rhyme be ragged,
> Tattered and jagged,
> Rudely rain-beaten,
> Rusty and moth-eaten,
> If ye take well therewith,
> It hath in it some pith.
> For, as far as I can see,
> It is wrong with each degree.

Skelton's kind of "bad" poetry has come to be called *Skeltonics*. Try to write a few lines of Skeltonic poetry. Make it in the voice of someone introducing herself or himself.

47

In this poem, called "A Wish," Samuel Rogers wishes he could live outside, next to a hill:

> Mine be a cot beside the hill;
> A bee-hive's hum shall soothe my ear;
> A willowy brook, that turns a mill,
> With many a fall shall linger near.
>
> The swallow oft beneath my thatch
> Shall twitter from her clay-built nest;
> Oft shall the pilgrim lift the latch
> And share my meal, a welcome guest.

48

Write a poem about an outside place in which you wish you could live—on a cloud, in the forest, on an iceberg, next to a hot spring, anywhere. What would you hear there? Who would visit you? What would you do together?

Write a poem about something that is usually unpleasant but in which you have found joy. You might want to think about a long car ride, waking up very early, a freezing cold day, or an unexpected rain shower. Try to include images that describe the scene and its beauty.

This poem by John Wilmot is about wanting to be something other than human:

> Were I (who to my cost already am
> One of those strange, prodigious creatures, man)
> A spirit free to choose, for my own share,
> What case of flesh and blood I pleased to wear,
> I'd be a dog, a monkey, a bear,
> Or anything but that vain animal
> Who is so proud of being rational. . . .

50

Wilmot hates that humans always have to be rational and thinking creatures. Have you ever wished you could choose another "case of flesh and blood?" Write a poem about what you would rather be, and why. Try to say what is most difficult about being a human and how that would be resolved if you were something else.

Write a poem that expresses a complete idea in only three words. It might help to write down a sentence about an experience you've had, and then condense it into three words that can explain the idea. For example: bubble floating pop. Or: holding carefully spilling.

51

The *haiku* is a Japanese form of poetry. A haiku is only three lines long, but it describes a whole scene or idea or a feeling that the poet has. Every haiku has 17 syllables: five in the first line, seven in the second, and five in the third. Haikus often describe images from nature. Here is an example of a haiku:

> Arched back, bent head, YAWN!
> My cat looks suddenly wild.
> But then he just sleeps.

Write a haiku about an animal, person, or scene.

52

Write a poem to an invention that you could never live without. Write it as if it is a love poem to the object, and try to make it funny. For example:

> O Internet! You reach me with a million web sites.
> Without you, how could I talk to my friends?
> (My father says, "Whatever happened to the phone?")
> But I love your flashing boxes and special offers.
> I never knew how special I was until I clicked on you.

53

Write a poem that scares you. It can be Hallowe'en-spooky or about a topic that makes you feel afraid, even if other people wouldn't be scared by it.

Daily Warm-Ups: Poetry

54

Write down five objects you can see from your desk. Now, write a poem that includes all of them, but in a setting that is not the classroom. You might want to imagine a strange room, place, or island that they have come from. For example (the five objects are in bold):

Reading Zoo

The **poster** says READ and that's what everyone is doing
the zebras
the monkeys
the hippopotami.
The zookeeper walks around with his **pencil,** making a mark in
    a **notebook**
when he finds that the lazy sloth is slacking again.
The sloth raises a slow eyelid and feels guilty,
    takes out his **book,** and gives a half- hearted
    leaf through the pages.
The zookeeper takes out his **eraser** and rubs,
    doubtingly.

55

© 2003 J. Weston Walch, Publisher

What is your favorite thing to do on the first day of summer vacation? Write a poem in which you explain how to make that day great. Write it as if you are giving directions, like this:

> Stay up late the night before.
> Go to bed only if your parents make you.
> Eat a quick breakfast of cereal and then run out to the pool
> Meet your friends for soccer in the afternoon . . .

This kind of poem, in which you are giving directions by using words like *stay, go, eat, run, meet,* is called *imperative*.

56

Write a line or a poem in which you string together words in a way you're sure no one's ever done before. Here's an example:

> Dancing in the mud
> the worm did a twist without meaning
> got lost
> and pushed its head forward to slide home, nearly missing
> the little worm hut.

57

Write a poem with five verbs and two nouns—and as few
other words as possible. For example:

> She pleaded
> asked
> demanded
> needed
> to possess
> a lollipop.

Daily Warm-Ups: Poetry

58

Daily Warm-Ups: Poetry

➤ *Goes with exercise 60*

A *ballad* is a poem that tells a story and was originally sung as a song. They were easy to remember and could be sung by people who could not read or write. They usually have four-line stanzas and a simple pattern of rhyme or repetition. Here is the first half of a ballad called "Lord Randal." Read it and then write down what would make the poem easy to remember and retell.

"O, where have you been, Lord Randal, my son?
O where have you been, my handsome young man?"—
　　"I have been to the wild wood; mother, make my bed soon,
　　For I'm weary with hunting, and fain would lie down."

"Who gave you your dinner, Lord Randal, my son?
Who gave you your dinner, my handsome young man?"—
　　"I dined with my sweetheart; mother, make my bed soon,
　　For I'm weary with hunting, and fain would lie down."

"What had you for dinner, Lord Randal, my son?
What had you for dinner, my handsome young man?"—
　　"I had eels boiled in broth; mother, make my bed soon,
　　For I'm weary with hunting, and fain would lie down."

59

➤ *Goes with exercise 59*

Read the second half of "Lord Randal":

"And where are your bloodhounds, Lord Randal, my son?
And where are your bloodhounds, my handsome young man?"—
　"O they swelled and they died; mother, make my bed soon,
　For I'm weary with hunting, and fain would lie down."

"O I fear you are poisoned, Lord Randal, my son!
O I fear you are poisoned, my handsome young man!"—
　"O yes! I am poisoned; mother, make my bed soon,
　For I'm sick at the heart, and fain would lie down."

Write a few sentences explaining what happened to Lord Randal. Then write your own ballad featuring someone who is trying to find out what happened to someone else. You can use a back-and-forth dialogue, as in "Lord Randal." Try to use four-line stanzas.

Write a poem about the first time you saw something that is now familiar to you—a younger sibling, a new home, a gift, a friend's house. Think about what kind of day it was, how the thing appeared to you then, and how you came to see the thing.

Write a poem that introduces an object and then lists everything the object could possibly be used for. Be imaginative in thinking about uses for your object. You may want to start: "A _____ is good for _____" and then continue your list. Here's an example:

> A jar is good for holding jam
> Catching fireflies
> Drinking if you have a wide mouth
> Rolling into pins when you've lost your bowling balls . . .

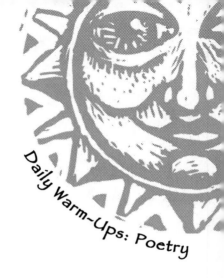

62

A *concrete poem* is one in which the poem's shape or the way it looks is important to the way we experience it. For example, a poem that is written in a circle will make us think about circles before we even read the words. The content of a concrete poem is usually related to its shape.

Write a concrete poem using a simple shape, such as a square, circle, or swirl. Here is an example of a square-shaped concrete poem:

The dog walks in a straight line.

The	owner
pulls	pulls
pulls	at his
leash	until

the dog agrees he will go home.

63

A.E. Housman wrote a poem about how well-behaved he became when he was in love with and trying to impress a certain woman:

> Oh, when I was in love with you,
>   Then I was clean and brave,
> And miles around the wonder grew
>   How well did I behave.
>
> And now the fancy passes by,
>   And nothing will remain
> And miles around they'll say that I
>   Am quite myself again.

64

At the end of the poem, Housman seems glad to be out of love—for the "fancy" or liking to have passed—since now he is himself again. Write a poem about something that changed your behavior, either for better or for worse, and how it felt when you returned to normal. You may want to use Housman's form:

When I was _____, then I was _____,
And now _____.

This is part of Elizabeth Barrett Browning's poem "The Cry of the Children," in which she wrote about the terrible working conditions of children in Victorian England:

> Go out, children, from the mine and from the city,
>   Sing out, children, as the little thrushes do;
> Pluck your handfuls of the meadow-cowslips pretty.
>   Laugh aloud, to feel your fingers let them through!
> But they answer . . .
> "Leave us quiet in the dark of the coal shadows,
>   From your pleasures fair and fine!"

> "For oh," say the children, "we are weary,
>   And we cannot run or leap;
> If we cared for any meadows, it were merely
>   To drop down in them and sleep. . . .
> For, all day, we drag our burden tiring
>   Through the coal-dark, underground;
> Or, all day, we drive the wheels or iron
>   In the factories, round and round."

65

Write a poem in which you describe an injustice in the world, aiming to expose it and get people angry enough to stop it.

If you had to give one piece of advice to your whole class, what would it be? Marcus Garvey wrote an advice poem telling everyone to "Keep Cool":

> . . . Let no trouble worry you;
> Keep cool, keep cool!
> Don't get hot like some folk do,
> Keep cool, keep cool!
> What's the use of prancing high
> While the world goes smiling by.
> You can win if you would try,
> Keep cool, keep cool.

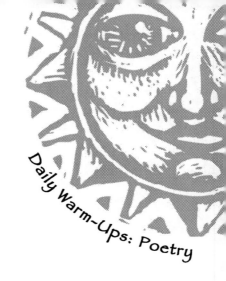

66

Write a poem containing a simple piece of advice. You may want to give it a rhythm, the way Garvey did, or make it sound like an advertisement or jingle.

Write a poem that is a dialogue between two people. To make it interesting, imagine one person has to tell the other something unexpected or disappointing. As you write the dialogue, think about what makes a poem dialogue different from one that is in a story.

Dora Greenwell wrote a poem called "Reconciliation" that begins with this image of sleep:

> Our waking hours write bitter things
> > Against us on Life's wall;
> But Sleep her small soft finger brings,
> > And draws it through them all.
> Oh! sweet her kiss on tired eyes,
> > More sweet to make amends
> Her child-kiss on the soul that lies,
> > And sayeth, 'Come, be friends!'

68

Greenwell personifies sleep, or imagines it as a person, one who calms the troubles of the day. By describing sleep as having "small soft finger[s]" and a "child-kiss," we get the sense that sleep is something young and innocent. Write a poem in which you imagine sleep as some kind of being. Try to think of exact images, the way Greenwell does. You might want to ask yourself the following: How big are Sleep's hands? How does Sleep put you to sleep? Is Sleep a young being or an old one? Male or female?

The word "squash" can mean three different things. As a noun, squash can be a game like racquetball, or it can be a vegetable (pumpkin is a squash). As a verb, it means to mash, crush, or squeeze. When you hear the word "squash," which do you think of first? Which definition sounds the "squashiest" to you? Write it down and explain why, and why the other two do not sound "squashy."

69

© 2003 J. Weston Walch, Publisher

Read this excerpt of a poem called "Answer Me" by Adah Isaacs Menken:

> The Storm struggles with the Darkness.
> Folded away in your arms, how little do I heed their battle!
> The trees clash in vain their naked swords against the door.
> I go not forth while the low murmur of your voice is drifting
>   all else back to silence.
> The darkness presses his black forehead close to the window
>   pane, and beckons me without.
> Love holds a lamp in this little room that hath the power to blot back Fear.

70

Imagery is a term used to describe things that we can imagine experiencing with our senses. Sometimes a poem contains imagery that creates a picture in our heads; maybe when you read the line "The darkness presses his black forehead close to the window pane" you could imagine the black night seeming to close in around you. Imagery is often expressed with similes and metaphors or personification. Some other images in the poem above are "The Storm struggles with the Darkness," "The trees clash in vain their naked swords against the door," and "Love holds a lamp in this little room."

Write a few lines about being home on a dark and stormy night. Use imagery to express how the night feels and what you see and hear.

Daily Warm-Ups: Poetry

Imagine a door that leads to a place no one has been for 500 years. Write a poem about what the door looks like, what it feels like to open it, and what you find on the other side.

71

Read part of "Song of Myself," by Walt Whitman, in which the speaker is inviting the reader to come and discover the world:

Have you reckon'd a thousand acres much? Have you reckon'd the
    earth much?
Have you practis'd so long to learn to read?
Have you felt so proud to get at the meaning of poems?

Stop this day and night with me and you shall possess the origin of
    all poems,
You shall possess the good of the earth and sun, (there are millions of
    suns left,)
You shall no longer take things at second or third hand, nor look through the
    eyes of the dead, nor feed on the specters in books,
      You shall not look through my eyes either, nor take things from me,
        You shall listen to all sides and filter them from your self.

72

Write a poem in which you invite someone to come on a journey to feel and learn all sorts of good and fantastic things. You can use the form that Whitman did: first ask "Have you . . ." about things that you have done that feel satisfying and magical, then "You shall . . ." about what lies in store on your journey.

Pick an object out of your desk or bag, or choose one that you can see inside the classroom or out the window. Think of surprising ways to describe the object without saying what it really is. Try to compare it to other objects, real or imagined. Make a list poem with the descriptions. Don't say what the object is except in the title of the poem, and try not to write "it looks like." Here is an example:

> **Pink Eraser**
> a chunk of bubble gum
> a pillow for a pixie's tiny head
> a bouncing ball with too many corners.

73

This is another part of Walt Whitman's "Song of Myself":

A child said *What is the grass?* fetching it to me with full hands,
How could I answer the child? I do not know what it is any more
than he.

I guess it must be the flag of my disposition, out of the hopeful green
stuff woven.
Or I guess it is the handkerchief of the Lord,
A scented gift and remembrancer designedly dropt,
Bearing the owner's name someway in the corners, that we may see and
remark, and say *Whose?*

Or I guess the grass is itself a child, the produced babe of vegetation.

Daily Warm-Ups: Poetry

74

Choose some element of the earth or sky—clouds, snow, air, soil, sea, etc.—and write a poem like Whitman's. Have someone ask you what the element is, and then answer in creative, imaginative ways, like Whitman. You could imagine that you have never seen the element before to generate some interesting possibilities. For example, "I guess a cloud is a floating bowl of milk. . . ."

Here is what is in Miranda's pockets: a sparkly green rock, a chewed up pencil, a key. Write a poem about Miranda and what the objects mean to her or what she does with them.

75

Think of your favorite drawing, photograph, or painting, one that you can picture in your head. Write a poem from it. You can either describe what it is, or write in a way that is similar to the style of the artwork. For example, a poem about a painting with lots of bright colors could either name the colors or use very bright and lively words.

76

Write a poem that describes a room in a way that makes it sound sad. There shouldn't be any people in the room—only objects or things like light, a breeze, or sounds. Try to be imaginative in the way that you describe the objects. You can personify them (make them like "persons"), using verbs or feelings that would normally be used for human beings. For example, "the hard wood chair was waiting with thin arms for a body that would never come."

77

© 2003 J. Weston Walch, Publisher

Sometimes in poetry, a specific detail, even if it seems small or minor, can express a lot about the emotion or scene described. For example, read these few lines about soldiers leaving their homes for battle, from "The Eve of Waterloo" by George Gordon, Lord Byron:

> Ah! then and there was hurrying to and fro,
>   And gathering tears, and tremblings of distress,
>   And cheeks all pale, which but an hour ago
>   Blushed at the praise of their own loveliness . . .

78

Instead of describing the entire scene, Byron uses a few key images to let us know that the goodbyes are quick and upsetting: "gathering tears," "tremblings of distress," "cheeks all pale." Those images let us sense the emotion of the scene, and even its action, in just a few lines. Now, you try it: write a few lines describing a scene of hurrying, and use specific, detailed images to convey the excitement or dread or quickness of the scene. You can set the scene quickly (for example: "'We will now begin boarding,' says the announcer") and then let your images explain the rest. Here are some images to get you thinking: hands clasping goodbye, a cap pulled down tight against the head, a suddenly dropped purse, a head turned back for one more "I'll miss you."

Write a poem describing the best thing you've ever tasted.
Make each line short, following the taste as it entered and left your
mouth. For example:

> Cold on my tongue
> Mint
> Not like toothpaste
> Cool and smooth and creamy
> A chocolate chip in the middle of my tongue
> It melts and is almost too sweet
> But the mint hurries it along, soothes my mouth . . .

79

Think of something that usually comes in a group: a bunch of bananas, a box of strawberries, a bouquet of flowers, an order of french fries. Write a poem imagining just one of the group in which you explain exactly what it looks, feels, or smells like and what makes it unique. Here's an example:

My french fry hangs over the others like a bendy-straw.
At first I think it'll be a soggy one.
But when I pull it out, it is long and graceful, perfectly golden.
The end is crispy brown.
It scoops up the ketchup like a parent lifting a small child.
In my mouth it feels so delicious
I don't even taste the bent part.

80

Mary Mollineux wrote a poem to her friend when she hadn't gotten a letter from her in a while. She wonders what it is that has kept her friend from writing, whether she is sick or has a new friend, and asks that she write to explain herself:

> Ah! Canst thou think what Doubtings do attend,
> Whether sad Sickness, or some rival Friend
> May now so long restrain thy careless Pen,
> As if it would not deign to write again?
> Or must that Friendship in Oblivion lie,
> That seems Immortal? Then send Reasons why:
> How should I else resent this Injury?

A poem that is a letter is called an *epistle*. Write an epistle to a friend in which you ask a question or make a demand. Or, invent two characters who are friends and have one write an epistle to the other.

81

Write a poem about what you wish would happen this afternoon. You can start every line with "I wish . . ." but the lines do not need to be complete sentences.

82

Write a poem about the best view you have ever seen from a window.

Daily Warm-Ups: Poetry

83

John Donne's poem "The Sun Rising" starts with the speaker complaining to the bright sun that he does not want to get out of bed:

> Busy old fool, unruly Sun,
> Why dost thou thus,
> Through windows and through curtains call on us?

How do you feel when you first open your eyes in the morning? Are you angry at the day for interrupting your sleep or eager to get into it? Write a poem about your first thoughts and feelings when you wake up. You might want to address the thing that wakes you directly, as Donne speaks to the sun, like this: "Beep, beep, beep! Stupid alarm, why do you blare at me? Snooze, please!"

*Daily Warm-Ups: Poetry*

84

Later in "The Sun Rising," Donne talks about how powerful he feels his sweetheart is, and how powerful he feels when he is with her:

> She's all States, and all Princes I;
> Nothing else is.

Donne says that his sweetheart is as powerful as all states (or nations), and that he is like all princes; he feels that there is nothing that can rival them. Notice that Donne makes the comparison by just saying that "She's all States," not that she is like all states or as powerful as all states. That kind of direct comparison of two unlike things is called a *metaphor*.

Write three metaphors about feeling powerful. Try to think of a moment when you felt really powerful, and what that could be compared to. Remember not to use like or as. Here are three examples:

- I am a spaceship pushing out to the atmosphere.

- I am a cowboy on top of a leaping horse.

- I am a thunderstorm making everyone run inside.

85

© 2003 J. Weston Walch, Publisher

Write a poem in which you apologize to something or someone.

86

Thomas Gray wrote a poem called "Ode on the Death of a Favourite Cat Drowned in a Tub of Gold Fishes." Here is the part of the poem when the cat sees the fish ("The Genii of the stream") and falls in:

> Still had she gazed; but 'midst the tide
> Two angel forms were seen to glide
>   The Genii of the stream:
> Their scaly armour's Tyrian hue
> Through richest purple to the view
>   Betrayed a golden gleam.
> The hapless nymph with wonder saw:
> A whisker first and then a claw,
>   With many an ardent wish,
> She stretched in vain to reach the prize.
> What female heart can gold despise?
>   What cat's averse to fish?

87

Notice how slowly Gray narrates the event, as if we are watching it in slow motion and considering every part of the cat sitting, watching the fish, reaching for them, and falling in. The slowness makes the cat's drowning suspenseful and dramatic. Write a poem about a time when you fell down, narrating it in slow motion. Try to include every detail that you saw, smelled, thought, or felt. You can start at the moment of falling or just before.

© 2003 J. Weston Walch, Publisher

Remember, a metaphor is a comparison of two essentially unlike things, like a simile, written by saying that one thing is the other. For example, "The sun is an egg yolk this morning." Fill in the blanks below to create imaginative, descriptive metaphors. You can extend the metaphors if you like; in the example above, an extended metaphor might be, "The sun is an egg yolk this morning, dropped into the bowl of the sky without a speck of shell."

The window is _____.

My family is _____.

A mountain is _____.

The fog is _____.

My personality is _____.

88

Freewriting is an exercise that many poets use when they feel blank about what to write. The idea of freewriting is that you start writing (sometimes while thinking of a sentence or idea or piece of music or art) and keep writing for a set amount of time. You can write the first thing that comes to mind—it doesn't have to be in full sentences or well thought-out—but you aren't supposed to pick up your pen from the paper to think. You just keep writing. Sometimes freewriting helps you get in the mood of writing, other times you might end up saying something that will be a good idea for a poem or story.

Freewrite for three minutes. If you're stuck for ideas, you can start with this sentence: "The air in the room changed suddenly."

89

This is the poem "The New Colossus" by Emma

Lazarus, which is inscribed on the Statue of Liberty.

Not like the brazen giant of Greek fame,
With conquering limbs astride from land to land;
Here at our sea-washed, sunset gates shall stand
A mighty woman with a torch, whose flame
Is the imprisoned lightning, and her name
Mother of Exiles. From her beacon-hand
Glows world-wide welcome; her mild eyes command
The air-bridged harbor that twin cities frame.
"Keep ancient lands, your storied pomp!" cries she
With silent lips. "Give me your tired, your poor,
Your huddled masses, yearning to breathe free,
The wretched refuse of your teeming shore.
Send these, the homeless, tempest-tost to me,
I lift my lamp beside the golden door!"

90

Imagine that you have been commissioned to write a new poem for the Statue of Liberty. How would you welcome immigrants into the United States?

Write a poem explaining what you had for breakfast. Imagine that the audience of your poem is a Martian who can understand you but doesn't know what foods we have on earth. In other words, don't just say you had oatmeal, write about the thick grayish mush that stuck to your spoon and throat.

91

Poets sometimes refer to their poems as "rhymes," as in "nursery rhymes." In one poem, Shakespeare wrote:

> Not marble, or the gilded monuments
> Of princes, shall outlive this powerful rhyme.

He believed that nothing would live longer than, or "outlive," his poem—not marble or a palace. What do you have that you want to live forever? Write a poem about how long it will last. You might want to start by filling in the blanks: My _____ will be here after _____ or, Nothing will last longer than _____, not even _____.

Daily Warm-Ups: Poetry

92

Percy Bysshe Shelley wrote a poem about an ancient king named Ozymandias, who was great and powerful. A traveler found a sculpture of him in the desert, all crumbled and decayed. There was a plaque by the ruins that said:

> My name is Ozymandias, king of kings:
> Look on my works, ye Mighty, and despair!

But of course, nothing is left from the king's works, not even the sculpture of himself. He felt he would be powerful forever, but every piece of him is gone or fallen.

Can you think of something that seems like it will last forever, but really won't? Maybe a day of school, or the summer, or a snowstorm? Write a poem about that thing and what it feels like when it is finally over.

93

Sir Edward Dyer wrote a poem about how he is happy living in the kingdom of his mind, or his imagination. Here is part of it:

> My mind to me a kingdom is
>   Such perfect joy therein I find,
> That it excels all other bliss
> That world affords or grows by kind.

Imagine a kingdom inside your mind. What does it look like? Who rules it? Who is in there? What kind of joy is there? Write a poem about it.

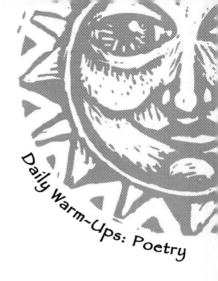

94

Write a poem about a secret inside place. Think broadly—it could be inside a box, inside your hand, or inside a pool.

95

Write a poem about a secret outside place. It can be outside of anything—your house, your family, your school.

96

A ***caricature*** in poetry, as in art, distorts a person's appearance and personality in a humorous way. Read a few verses of a caricature poem Edward Lear wrote about himself, "How pleasant to know Mr. Lear." He wrote it as if he were talking about someone else:

> How pleasant to know Mr. Lear!
> > Who has written such volumes of stuff!
> Some think him ill-tempered and queer,
> > But a few think him pleasant enough.
>
> His mind is concrete and fastidious,
> > His nose is remarkably big;
> His visage is more or less hideous,
> > His beard it resembles a wig.

Write a caricature poem about yourself. You can use "he" or "she" instead of "I," the way Lear did.

97

© 2003 J. Weston Walch, Publisher

Think of a section in the library or bookstore: science fiction, self-help, poetry, etc. Then write a poem that is a list of books in the section. Make the titles as crazy as possible. For example, here's the beginning of a poem called "How-to books":

> 600 More Ways to Make Eggs
>
> How to Sweat Without Showing It
>
> Crayons for Grown-Ups
>
> Are You Double-Jointed?

98

Close your eyes and think of the word "bowl." Write a poem about the image or images that you see.

99

Phillis Wheatley wrote a poem called "To S.M., A Young African Painter, On Seeing His Works." As you read the beginning of it, pay attention to how amazed and impressed she is with the painter's ability to create lifelike people.

> To show the lab'ring bosom's deep intent,
> And thought in living characters to paint,
> When first thy pencil did those beauties give,
> And breathing figures learnt from thee to live,
> How did those prospects give my soul delight,
> A new creation rushing on my sight?

Think of a time when you encountered a piece of art that impressed you—a film, book, painting, photograph, sculpture, anything. Then write a poem to the artist explaining what you found most amazing. Try to capture the sense of wonder that Wheatley does in the last two lines.

100

Pick a random object. Describe a parent or sibling or friend by making comparisons to that object. For example: object = tennis racquet; person = Mom.

My mother is bigger than a tennis racquet, but just as graceful.
When she dances she swings like a racquet
Sometimes she is angry like a racquet with a popped string,
　　she doesn't want to do anything.

101

© 2003 J. Weston Walch, Publisher

Frances Sargent Osgood wrote a poem called "Ellen Learning to Walk" about her daughter's first steps. Read a few verses, paying attention to how Osgood conveys the excitement of the moment and her pride:

> My beautiful trembler! how wildly she shrinks
>   And how wistful she looks while she lingers!
> Papa is extremely uncivil, she thinks,—
>   She but pleaded for one of his fingers! . . .
>
> Come on, my pet Ellen! we won't let you slip,—
>   Unclasp those soft arms from his knee, love;
> I see a faint smile round that exquisite lip,
> A smile half reproach and half glee, love….
>
> There! steady my darling! huzza! I have caught her!
>   I clasp her, caress'd and caressing!
> And she hides her bright face, as if what we had taught her
>   Were something to blush for—the blessing!

Now write a poem about watching something that makes you feel proud. Try to narrate the scene slowly, the way Osgood does, so that the final event feels like a real accomplishment.

Read these lines by Thomas Hardy:

> Childlike, I danced in a dream;
> Blessings emblazoned that day;
> Everything glowed with a gleam;
> Yet we were looking away!

Do you see or hear the way that there are lots of "d" sounds in the first line, "b" sounds in the second, "g" sounds in the third, and "w" sounds in the fourth? A repeated sound in a series of words is called *alliteration*. Using the first sound in your name, write a poem that contains alliteration. You don't need to put the sound in every word, but you should be able to hear it as the main sound if you read the poem aloud.

103

© 2003 J. Weston Walch, Publisher

Assonance is the repetition of a vowel sound in a sequence of words. For example, most of the words in this line have the same short "I" sound as in the word "sit": Sitting himself down in the pit, he hid quickly. Write two lines that contain assonance.

104

William Cullen Bryant's poem "The Prairies" talks about prairies as a uniquely American landscape:

> These are the gardens of the Desert, these
> The unshorn fields, boundless and beautiful,
> For which the speech of England has no name—
> The Prairies. I behold them for the first,
> And my heart swells, while the dilated sight
> Takes in the encircling vastness. Lo! they stretch,
> In airy undulations, far away,
> As if the ocean, in his gentlest swell,
> Stood still, with all his rounded billows fixed,
> And motionless forever.

Write a poem about a landform, landscape, streetscape, or type of building that is unique to where you live. Try to make a comparison that will help someone who has never seen the place before understand it, the way that Bryant imagines the prairies as the rolling ocean standing still. You can start your poem by saying, "Only in _____ have I seen _____" and then describing what the place is like.

105

➤ *Goes with exercise 107*

Write a good-bye poem. Say good-bye to someone who is leaving, and try to include some details about what the separation will be like: Why is the other person leaving? For how long will he or she be gone? Is he or she excited or sad to be leaving, and how does that make you feel?

106

➤ *Goes with exercise 106*

Read the good-bye poem you wrote to yourself.

Imagine the speaker of the poem. Is the speaker comfortable, sitting with a glass of lemonade in the back yard, or in a rush, about to run out of the house? Think about what the speaker's voice sounds like. Is the speaker angry, happy, or upset? Is the speaker thinking about everything that is being said and talking slowly, or just saying the first thing that comes to mind?

Now, write the good-bye poem again but with a different voice. If your first voice was sad, can you find an angry way to say good-bye? A careless way? A cheerful way?

107

© 2003 J. Weston Walch, Publisher

Write a poem that is all lies. It can be about you or the world in general.

108

Have you ever wanted to protect something? Anything—a younger brother or sister, or a sand castle on the beach? This is part of a poem by Shakespeare that tells certain animals to stay away from the fairy queen:

> You spotted snakes with double tongue,
> Thorny hedgehogs, be not seen;
> Newts and blind-worms, do no wrong;
> Come not near our fairy queen.

Think of something you'd like to protect and write a poem saying what must stay away from it. It could be real things like this: Heavy waves, don't come near my sand fortress. Or it could be ideas: Nightmares, spooky visions, keep away from my mind as I'm falling asleep.

109

Here are five words: bread, violet, swing, glow, fan.

Pick one and write a poem using it as the title.

110

D.H. Lawrence wrote a poem remembering how his mother would play the piano for his family. Here is part of it:

> The full throated woman has chosen a winning, living song
> And surely the heart that is in me must belong
> To the old Sunday evenings, when darkness wandered outside
> And hymns gleamed on our warm lips, as we watched mother's
>   fingers glide.

What do you think Lawrence meant by "And surely the heart that is in me must belong/To the old Sunday evenings"? Write a poem about the place or time to which the heart in you belongs. Is it with your family on a holiday? Or with your friends after school?

111

The *theme* of the poem is the subject that it deals with, or the idea about the world that it expresses. Write a poem in which the theme has to do with falling.

112

Choose one poem you've already written for this

exercise. *Narrative poems* (those that tell a story) will work well. Then, take another poem and give it to someone near you. You should end up with one poem that you wrote and one that someone else wrote. Now, write a poem by combining the two poems. You can alternate words, lines, or stanzas, or change around the order of one or both poems, or just put words from someone else's poems in your own. Try to make the new poem funny or silly.

113

Write a poem about something in which you believe. Include any evidence or experiences that have led you to this belief. You may want to include another voice, questioning your belief, and your answer.

114

Write a poem describing the first thought that comes to your mind when you read the word *vacation*. The thought should be about something you experience with your senses, but it doesn't have to be visual; it could be a smell, the temperature of the air, or the taste of a certain food.

115

© 2003 J. Weston Walch, Publisher

At the end of a poem called "To Althea, from Prison," in which the speaker is writing to his love from jail, Richard Lovelace writes:

> Stone walls do not a prison make,
>   Nor iron bars a cage;
> Minds innocent and quiet take
>   That for an hermitage;
> If I have freedom in my love,
>   And in my soul am free;
> Angels alone that soar above
>   Enjoy such liberty.

116

Write down your answers to the following: What does Lovelace mean by the first two lines, "Stone walls do not a prison make, Nor iron bars a cage"? What does make a prison or a cage? What allows the speaker in the poem to be free?

Think about different ways to emphasize words in your writing. You could write all in CAPITALS. You could repeat, repeat, repeat the word. You could use strong punctuation! You could also rhyme every word except the one you want to stand out, or make every word start with the same letter except the one you want to emphasize.

Write three different lines or sentences in which the word "still" is emphasized in three different ways. You can think of "still" as meaning either "not moving" or "yet."

117

Shakespeare wrote a poem about a fairy who can sleep or ride or go in any fantastic place. Read it. (A "cowslip" is a yellow flower and its "bell" is the tiny cup-like part of it.)

Where the bee sucks, there suck I,
In a cowslip's bell I lie,
There I couch when owls do cry,
On the bat's back I do fly
After summer merrily.
    Merrily, merrily, shall I live now
    Under the blossom that hangs on the bough.

118

Is there a small or secret place where you would like to live? What animal or airplane or spaceship would you like to fly on? Write a poem in which you pretend that you can be in these magical places. You can also have other superpowers or abilities if you wish.

If a secret were something you could hold, where would you hide yours? Elizabeth Barrett Browning writes about a room that seems as if it could hide nothing:

> 'Twas a room
> Scarce larger than a grave, and near as bare;
> Two stools, a pallet bed; I saw the room:
> A mouse could find no sort of shelter in't,
> Much less a greater secret; curtainless,—
> The window fixed you with its torturing eye . . .

Invent a room which is the opposite of Browning's—one in which you could hide lots of things—creatures, friends, secrets, etc. Write a poem describing its mysterious compartments, trick doors, thick curtains, and anything else that makes it a good secret-keeper.

119

© 2003 J. Weston Walch, Publisher

Walt Whitman wrote about a child who identifies with objects that he sees:

> There was a child went forth every day,
> And the first object he look'd upon, that object he became,
> And that object became a part of him for the day or a certain
>   part of the day,
> Or for many years or stretching cycles of years.

Can you remember the first object you saw this morning? Write a poem imagining how you have become that object or how it has become a part of you. For example, if you woke up to the sun, maybe you have been shining and bright today; if you woke to an alarm clock, maybe you have been noisy. You may want to begin by filling in the blanks: This morning I saw _____ and now I am _____. If you'd like, you can use long, flowy lines the way Whitman does.

120

Samuel Johnson wrote this celebratory poem when his friend turned 21:

> Long-expected one-and-twenty,
> Lingering year at last is flown:
> Pomp and pleasure, pride and plenty,
> Great Sir John, are all your own . . .
>
> Call the Betties, Kates, and Jennies,
> Every name that laughs at care;
> Lavish of your grandsire's guineas,
> Show the spirit of an heir.

An *occasional poem* is one that is written to celebrate or commemorate an event such as a birthday, graduation, marriage, or death. Write an occasional poem for someone you know who has recently celebrated a birthday or anniversary. You may want to write about what the new year will bring, the way Johnson does.

121

Jam, orange, *switch, custom, free, cutting,* and *key* are some words that have at least two different meanings. Pick one of the words (or choose one of your own) and write two lines that contain the word. In each line the word should have a different meaning. Try to make the two lines related. For example:

I saw her newspaper cutting.
It was a cutting remark. I don't know why she saved it.

122

Write a poem about what you do and do not like about poems and poetry. You can call the poem "About Poetry" and start lines "I love . . ." or "It's fun to . . ." and "But I hate . . ." or "It's hard to . . .".

123

What is your earliest memory? Try to imagine that you have been taken back in time and put yourself at the scene of the memory. Is it an important event or just an ordinary day? What do you see, hear, smell? Who else is in the memory? Write a poem about the memory as if you are experiencing it. Use present tense verbs: I see . . ., she walks towards me . . . .

Daily Warm-Ups: Poetry

124

Jamaican poet W. Adolphe Roberts wrote this poem, called "The Maroon Girl." Notice how he seems to be watching the girl closely but without her knowing he is there:

> I see her on a lonely forest track,
> Her level brows made salient by the sheen
> Of flesh the hue of cinnamon . . .
> She is a peasant, yet she is a queen.
> She is Jamaica poised against attack.
> Her woods are hung with orchids, the still flame
> Of red hibiscus lights her path, and starred
> With orange and coffee blossoms is her yard.
> Fabulous, pitted mountains close the frame.
> She stands on ground for which her fathers died;
> Figure of savage beauty, figure of pride.

Choose someone in your class and watch him or her closely for about three minutes. Try to be secretive! Then write a poem in which you use metaphors and a setting to make the person seem powerful, the way Roberts did. For example: She's a basketball all-star, tightening the laces on brand-new shoes, about to burst onto the court to the sounds of screaming fans . . . .

125

© 2003 J. Weston Walch, Publisher

Have you heard the term *déjà vu*? In French, it means *already seen*, and it describes the feeling that you've already experienced something that you are experiencing. *Déjà vu* sometimes feels as if you once dreamt the exact scene that you find yourself in. Dante Gabriel Rossetti wrote "Sudden Light" about feeling a kind of *déjà vu* for a place he is in and a woman he sees:

> I have been here before,
> > But when or how I cannot tell:
> I know the grass beyond the door,
> > The sweet keen smell,
> The sighing sound, the lights around the shore.

> > You have been mine before,—
> > > How long ago I may not know:
> > But just when at that swallow's soar
> > > Your neck turned so,
> > Some veil did fall,—I knew it all of yore.

126

Write a poem about experiencing *déjà vu*. If you can't think of an actual incident, imagine one. Try to name the details that give you the *déjà vu* feeling—in Rossetti's poem, it is the grass that he knows will be behind the door and the shape of the woman's neck as she raises her head to follow a bird.

In a letter poem to Miss Blount, who left town to go off by herself, Alexander Pope imagined what she would be doing:

> She went from opera, park, assembly, play,
> To morning-walks, and prayers three hours a day,
> To part her time 'twixt reading and Bohea,
> To muse, and spill her solitary tea,
> Or o'er cold coffee trifle with the spoon;
> Count the slow clock, and dine exact at noon,
> Divert her eyes with pictures in the fire,
> Hum half a tune, tell stories to the squire. . . .

Write a poem about what you would do if you lived all alone. What and how would you eat and drink? Would you build a fire and see pictures in it? What would be fun about it? What would be lonely? You might want to pretend you've done it, and use Pope's basic form:

> I went from parents, school, and friends
> To bicycle riding, and eating chocolate for breakfast
> To watching long movies every night. . . .

127

Ask the person sitting next to you to tell you about something important that he or she is wearing or has in his or her bookbag or desk. Ask questions so that you really understand what the person's relationship is to the thing. For instance, if your neighbor is telling you about her new sneakers, you could ask: Who bought you the sneakers? How small were your old ones? Are the new ones good for running? Do they ever hurt your feet? Then write a poem about that person's object and relationship to it.

Daily Warm-Ups: Poetry

128

Alice Christiana Gertrude Meynell wrote a poem called "A Letter from a Girl to Her Own Old Age." Write a letter poem to your own old age. What advice would you give yourself? What memories would you want to recall when you are 75 years old? You may want to start your lines with, "Remember the time . . .," "Always act as if . . .," "Don't forget about . . .," "Now that you're a grown-up . . .".

129

Write an imperative poem that is your recipe for happiness. Think about what the ingredients are—maybe an afternoon with your best friend? A party with chocolate cake? A big surprise birthday present? Then think of how they should be mixed up or combined. Here are some verbs you may want to use: stir, shake, add, fold, beat, bake, freeze. Say how happiness should be served or eaten, too: with special silverware or fingers, on a picnic or in bed.

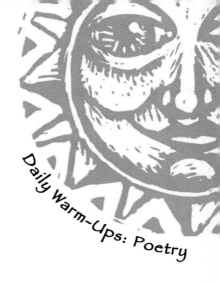

130

Do you ever think about publishing your poems, or giving them as gifts to your family and friends? In a poem to the West Wind, Percy Bysshe Shelley asks for his poem to be blown to all of mankind:

> Scatter, as from an unextinguished hearth
> Ashes and sparks, my words among mankind!
> Be through my lips to unawakened earth
>
> The trumpet of a prophecy!

Write a few lines or a poem about where you'd like to send your poems and why. Who do you think would like to read them? Can you think of a creative way to send them, the way that Shelley does—maybe across the sea in a bottle, or in a bird's beak, or on a ray of the sun?

131

When Shakespeare writes about what the month of April is like, he imagines that April is a being that makes things happen: " . . . April, dressed in all his trim . . . put a spirit of youth in every thing."

Write a poem which personifies your birthday month. Think about how it would be dressed and what it does. For example:

> July doesn't wear anything but a bathing suit
> exhausting us with so many hot days.
> July turns on the sprinklers and watches the kids
> running through the cold rainbow spray.

In a poem about a horse, William Shakespeare gives a detailed description of how it looks:

> Round-hoofed, short-jointed, fetlocks shag and long,
>   Broad breast, full eye, small head, and nostril wide,
> High crest, short ears, straight legs and passing strong,
>   Thin mane, thick tail, broad buttock, tender hide . . .

Think of an animal and write down a short phrase describing each part of it, the way Shakespeare does. For example, you might describe a cat like this: pointy ears, round eyes, twitching whiskers, fat belly, swooshing tail, tip-toe feet. See if the person next to you can guess which animal you wrote about just by the description.

133

Choose an object—a car, a violin, a refrigerator, a

salad—and imagine you've just turned into it. Write a poem about your new body. Where are your hands? Your bones? Your tongue? Your brain? Your feelings?

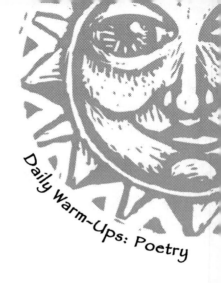

134

Alfred, Lord Tennyson wrote a poem in the voice of Ulysses, or Odysseus, who has just returned home after fighting in a war and having years of adventures at sea. He is bored and wants to figure out how to keep leading an adventurous life:

> How dull it is to pause, to make an end,
> To rust unburnished, not to shine in use!
> As though to breathe was life. . . .
> Come, my friends,
> 'Tis not too late to seek a newer world.
> Push off, and sitting well in order smite
> The sounding furrows; for my purpose holds
> To sail beyond the sunset, and the baths
> Of all the western stars, until I die. . . .

Have you ever returned from a really fun experience and been let down by normal life? Write a poem describing how you felt. Did you feel, like Ulysses, that all you were doing was breathing and not really living? At the end of the poem, call your friends or family to do something or go somewhere that will make you feel vibrant again.

135

Write a poem imagining that you are talking to someone famous. First set the scene. Is the person at the table next to you in a restaurant? Are you talking online? Did she show up at your house asking directions? Then write your conversation, describing what you say and how nervous you feel (or don't feel) as you're saying it. How does the famous person react? How will your memory of the encounter be different from the famous person's?

136

Abraham Lincoln wrote these lines in a poem called "My Childhood-Home I See Again."

> As distant mountains please the eye,
> When twilight chases the day—
> As bugle-tones, that, passing by,
> In distance die away—

Notice how he compares the sight of the sunset—"When twilight chases the day"—to the sound of the bugle dying away in the distance. Both the sight and the sound make us think of things that are slowly ending or going away from us. Now, think of a feeling—maybe winning a game, or being lost, or getting frustrated—and write down two ways to describe it, one using sight and one using sound.

137

What is your favorite color? Imagine you can touch, smell, taste, and hear it. Write down what it is like. Does it feel soft like a cotton ball or spiky like a cactus? Does it smell cozy like baking bread or sour like a lemon? Does it taste smooth like ice cream or crunchy like toast? Is it a big loud sound or a quiet whispering one?

138

Write a poem featuring a conversation you eavesdropped on. Make it like a scene, describing yourself and where you are, who you are listening to, how they are expressing themselves, and what you learn or guess. Here's an example:

"Well he is fat and you can tell he's getting older"
I turn my head. She's fat and you can tell she's getting older too.
The bus driver pulls to the curb
Woman next to me raises her eyebrows, high: can you believe her?
"His coat is not as shiny, either"
It's my stop
She's talking about her dog.

139

Do you ever feel regret, a feeling that you shouldn't have done something that you did, or that you should have done something you didn't? Paul Lawrence Dunbar wrote this poem about feeling regret before falling asleep:

> Ere sleep comes down to soothe the weary eyes
> How all the griefs and heartaches we have known
> Come up like pois'nous vapors that arise
> From some base witch's caldron, when the crone,
> To work some potent spell, her magic plies.
> The past which held its share of bitter pain,
> Whose ghost we prayed that Time might exorcise,
> Comes up, is lived and suffered o'er again,
> Ere sleep comes down to soothe the weary eyes.

140

Write a poem either about something you regret, or about how regret feels inside you. You can use Dunbar's language of vapors and ghosts, or create your own comparisons.

Write a poem that sounds like a newspaper article, reporting on something that you saw happen. Make it very factual. Then read it over and think about how you can change it by finding places to put your feelings or what went through your head. You might want to put these personal thoughts in parentheses.

Daily Warm-Ups: Poetry

141

Sometimes poets change around or alter words to more specifically express themselves. Ralph Waldo Emerson played with language in his poem "The Humble-Bee." The title is a play on the word "bumblebee" that he makes to describe the bee as humble. He also says that the bee is a "zigzag steerer, desert cheerer." Although "steerer" is not a real word, we understand that a "zigzag steerer" is one who steers in a zigzag way. Emerson's made-up word is very specific, which helps us understand how the bee moves.

Write down some things that you like to do, making them as specific and unique as possible—for example, drink vanilla soda, read a book with lots of pictures, see a long movie, play guitar, etc. Then create a poem uniquely about you by changing around the phrases to follow the words "I am a." For example,

I am a
Vanilla soda drinker
Picture book reader
Long movie seer
Guitar player . . .

142

Some poems don't rhyme at all; those that do can use different patterns or *rhyme schemes*. Here are two examples. In each stanza of the ballad "The Demon Lover," the second and fourth lines rhyme:

> She set her foot upon the ship—
> No mariners could she behold;
> But the sails were of the taffeta,
> And the masts of the beaten gold.

In Christopher Marlowe's "The Passionate Shepherd to His Love," the first two lines of each stanza and the last two rhyme:

> A gown made of the finest wool
> Which from our pretty lambs we pull;
> Fair lined slippers for the cold
> With buckles of the purest gold.

Make up a rhyme scheme, or pattern, for a four-line stanza. Write at least two stanzas using your rhyme scheme or one of the ones above.

143

© 2003 J. Weston Walch, Publisher

One-syllable words can be easy to rhyme: pie, eye, sky, dry, lie, etc. But what about rhyming words with more than one syllable? What rhymes with water? With turning? Rhyming just the last syllable won't really work; computer doesn't rhyme with water, skipping doesn't rhyme with turning.

John Dryden wrote a poem in which he rhymed the last two syllables of three long words: possessing, expressing, a blessing. Then, he rhymed three phrases the same way: descried it, beside it, has tried it. Can you think of two words that rhyme with "running"? Try to make them full rhymes like Dryden did—rhyming the "run" syllable and the "ing" syllable, not just the "ing." How about two words that rhyme with "broken" and two more for "butter"?

144

Imagine a suitcase left on a train platform. It is blue and square and very neat, except for something red sticking out from the side. It has no tags. There is a woman on a bench, waiting for something; she is near the suitcase, but it isn't hers. Write a poem about whose suitcase it is, what is inside, and how it got left there.

145

Christina Georgina Rossetti wrote this poem entitled "A Birthday":

My heart is like a singing bird
Whose nest is in a watered shoot;
My heart is like an apple-tree
    Whose boughs are bent with
      thickset fruit;
My heart is like a rainbow shell
That paddles in a halcyon sea;
My heart is gladder than all these
Because my love is come to me.

Raise me a dais of silk and
    down;
Hang it with vair and
    purple dyes;
Carve it in doves and
    pomegranates,
And peacocks with a hundred eyes;
Work it in gold and silver grapes,
In leaves and silver fleurs-de-lys;
Because the birthday of my life
Is come, my love is come to me.

Daily Warm-Ups: Poetry

146

Write a poem about your birthday. Use the form of Rossetti's poem—start with similes about how you feel (you can say "I am like . . ." instead of "My heart is like . . ." if it sounds better to you). Then give orders for a fabulous party with all sorts of decorations and food to celebrate.

Daily Warm-Ups: Poetry

In this poem by Emily Brontë, the speaker is a prisoner:

'Still let my tyrants know, I am not doomed to wear
Year after year in gloom, and desolate despair;
A messenger of Hope comes every night to me,
And offers for short life, eternal liberty.

'He comes with western winds, with evening's wandering airs,
With that clear dusk of heaven that brings the thickest stars,
Winds take a pensive tone, and stars a tender fire,
And visions rise, and change, that kill me with desire . . .'

Write a poem in the voice of someone from whom we don't
usually hear—a prisoner, a baby, or someone who lives alone on
a mountain, for example. Imagine that you are the person and
have something to say to the world. You may want to include a
surprising vision or idea the person has, the way Brontë does.

147

© 2003 J. Weston Walch, Publisher

Write a poem about your hands. Describe the way that they look and feel, and the markings or shape that make them unique.

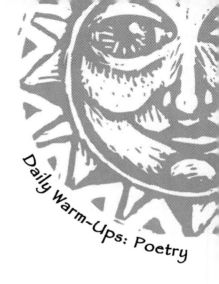

Daily Warm-Ups: Poetry

148

Here are two stanzas from a poem called "Sally in our Alley" by Henry Carey. As you read it, notice how the last two lines of each stanza are the same.

Of all the girls that are so smart
   There's none like pretty Sally;
She is the darling of my heart,
   And she lives in our alley.
There is no lady in the land
   Is half so sweet as Sally;
She is the darling of my heart,
   And she lives in our alley . . .

Of all the days that's in the week
I dearly love but one day—
   And that's the day that comes
     betwixt
A Saturday and Monday;
For then I'm drest in all my best
To walk abroad with Sally;
She is the darling of my heart,
   And she lives in our alley.

Repeated lines that continue through a poem are called the *refrain*. Write a poem or song that has a refrain. The poem can be about someone who lives near you who you've always liked or are curious about. You might want to model your refrain after Carey's by filling in the blanks: "_____ is _____, And _____ lives _____."

149

In "The Passionate Shepherd to His Love,"

Christopher Marlowe writes as if he is a shepherd asking his love to come away with him. Here is the beginning of it:

> Come live with me and be my love,
> And we will all the pleasures prove,
> That hills and valleys, dales and fields,
> And all the craggy mountains yields.
>
> There we will sit upon the rocks,
> And see the shepherds feed their flocks,
> By shallow rivers to whose falls
> Melodious birds sing madrigals.
>
> And I will make thee beds of roses
> With a thousand fragrant posies,
> A cap of flowers, and a kirtle
> Embroidered all with leaves of myrtle.

Daily Warm-Ups: Poetry

150

Write a poem in which you invite someone to go somewhere lovely and beautiful with you. It could be somewhere you've visited or a made-up place. Write about the pleasures that you will find there so that the person will really want to come along.

Jonathan Swift wrote a few poems in the voices of women selling things at a market. Here is one called "Onions":

> Come, follow me by the smell,
> Here are delicate onions to sell;
> I promise to use you well.
> They make the blood warmer,
> You'll feed like a farmer;
> For this is every cook's opinion,
> No savory dish without an onion;
> But, lest your kissing should be spoiled,
> Your onion must be thoroughly boiled . . .

Write a poem in which you are selling something. Choose an item that would be difficult to sell—a used toothbrush, a half-eaten ice cream cone, your socks—and make it funny, the way Swift does.

151

In a poem called "Frost at Midnight," Samuel Taylor Coleridge writes about how quiet the night is:

> 'Tis calm indeed! so calm, that it disturbs
> And vexes meditation with its strange
> And extreme silentness.

Write a poem about a "strange and extreme silentness." It might help to recall a time when you felt you were hearing the silence.

Daily Warm-Ups: Poetry

152

➤ *Goes with exercise 154*

Rhythm **in poetry,** like rhythm in music, is the pattern of strong sounds or beats we hear. In poetry, rhythm can be affected by the way that the words sound after each other, the beat that they follow, and whether the lines are long or short. You can write a rhythm that matches the subject of the poem, like Samuel Taylor Coleridge did in this passage from "Frost at Midnight":

> the thin blue flame
> Lies on my low-burnt fire, and quivers not;

Using so many one-syllable words after each other gives the feeling of the steady flame and the still night that Coleridge is describing. When the sentence changes—"and quivers not"—it makes us stop to think about how strong the flame must be, not to quiver in a disruptive way.

Write a poem about something that seems smooth to you—it could be an object, like your best old sweatshirt, or an activity, like swimming. Use words and a rhythm that match the smoothness of the subject.

153

© 2003 J. Weston Walch, Publisher

➤ *Goes with exercise 153*

Now, write a poem about something that is rough or hard, and create a rhythm that is also harsh. Think about using lots of clashing or difficult words in a row, like this:

> Raking with a cumbersome, broken, ungainly rake
> Forcing shrivelly leaves to pile . . . .

Daily Warm-Ups: Poetry

154

Read the poem "Snow-Flakes" by Henry Wadsworth Longfellow:

Out of the bosom of the Air,
Out of the cloud-folds of her
    garments shaken,
Over the woodlands brown and
    bare,
Over the harvest-fields
    forsaken,
Silent, and soft, and slow
Descends the snow.

Even as our cloudy fancies take
Suddenly shape in some divine
    expression,
Even as the troubled heart doth
    make
In the white countenance
    confession,
The troubled sky reveals
The grief it feels.

This is the poem of the air,
Slowly in silent syllables recorded;
This is the secret of despair,
Long in its cloudy bosom hoarded,
Now whispered and revealed
To wood and field.

Write a poem about snow. Try to express how it is "the poem of the air."

155

© 2003 J. Weston Walch, Publisher

Have you ever wondered what an animal or other creature thinks of you? For instance, what your dog thinks of the way you keep it on a leash and only feed it at certain times, or what a bug thinks when you step on it? Sarah Orne Jewett wonders what her pet bird thinks of her in "A Caged Bird":

> What can my life seem like to her?
> A dull, unpunctual service mine,
> Stupid before her eager call,
> Her flitting steps, her insight fine.
>
> To open wide thy prison door,
> Poor friend, would give thee to thy foes;
> And yet a plaintive note I hear,
> As if to tell how slowly goes
>
> The time of thy long prisoning . . . .

156

Write a poem in which you speak to a creature that might question the way you act, explaining yourself.

Daily Warm-Ups: Poetry

Write a poem by filling in the blanks. You may use as many words as you want in each blank, but try to keep the placement of the words as they appear below.

Traveling _____ without_____

_____curious_____orange

_____except_____

_____finally_____

Sweet_____exhausted.

157

Ralph Waldo Emerson wrote a poem called "Mithridates"—Mithridates was the name of a king who took poisons in small quantities to make himself immune to them. In the poem, Emerson writes about loving nature so much that he would eat every kind of natural thing.

Give me agates for my meat;
Give me cantharids to eat;
From air and ocean bring me foods,
From all zones and altitudes;—

From all natures, sharp and slimy,
Salt and basalt, wild and tame:
Tree and lichen, ape, sea-lion,
Bird, and reptile, be my game.

Write a poem about something you love so much you feel you could survive on it. Like Emerson, pretend you can eat or drink from it. Make your poem humorous, like Emerson's. For example:

All I need is soccer
I'll eat a shin guard for breakfast
And wash it down with a dirty black and white ball
For lunch a pair of just-washed shorts
For dinner my sweaty shirt . . . .

158

John Keats wrote a poem called "Ode on a Grecian Urn" (an ode is a long and lyrical poem that is usually about a serious subject). The Grecian urn has a scene carved or painted on it, and Keats talks to the elements of the scene as if they are real beings, frozen in time the way they were drawn. Here is part of his poem in which he addresses a piper (a young man playing a pipe) about to kiss a lady:

> Fair youth, beneath the trees, thou canst not leave
> Thy song, nor ever can those trees be bare;
> Bold Lover, never, never canst thou kiss,
> Though winning near the goal—yet, do not grieve;
> She cannot fade, though thou hast not thy bliss,
> For ever wilt thou love, and she be fair!

Find a photograph or piece of art with people in it and imagine they are frozen in the scene. They have whatever feelings and ideas they had when they were frozen, forever. Write a poem like Keats's in which you tell the people what is wonderful or terrible about where they are stuck. You can write questions to the people and tell them why you would or wouldn't want to be in the scene with them.

159

Write a short poem in which you announce something you are quite sure of but which people around you don't seem to know. For example:

> If young people were just allowed to vote
> or better yet, run for office,
> this country could be a lot more fun.

160

Here are "to be" verbs: am, are, is, was, were. They express something in a simple way; for example, "The fish is blue." What is another way to describe the color of the fish? You could say that the fish wears blue, or that it swims in blue skin, or that it shines with blue light, or that blue covers its body. Lines without "to be" verbs are usually more descriptive and interesting. Write a poem of at least four lines, without any "to be" verbs. The poem should describe a person or animal you know well. For an extra challenge, try not to use "have" or "has," either.

161

For this exercise, students should bring in the oldest family photograph they can find.

Oliver Wendell Holmes wrote a poem while looking at a family portrait of "Dorothy Q," who lived a hundred years before. In the poem, he describes what Dorothy looks like and then thinks about how, without her, he'd never have been born:

> O Damsel Dorothy! Dorothy Q!
> Strange is the gift that I owe to you;
> Such a gift as never a king
> Save to daughter or son might bring . . .
>
> What if a hundred years ago
> Those close-shut lips had answered No . . .
>
> Should I be I? . . .

162

Holmes wonders whether, if the woman in the portrait hadn't married the man she did ("had answered No"), he would exist as himself. Look at an old family photograph and write a poem in which you talk to someone in the picture. Ask the person questions about his or her life, relating it to your own if possible. For example, you could ask a great-grandparent, "What if you hadn't moved to America? Would I be living here now?" You might want to start by describing the photograph and how the person appears.

© 2003 J. Weston Walch, Publisher

Ivan Van Sertima wrote a poem in which he compares his anger to a volcano:

> When I speak now
> there are no urgent rumblings in my voice
> no scarlet vapour issues from my lips
> I spit no lava:
> but I am a volcano
> an incandescent cone of angry flesh
> black brimstone broils within
> the craters of my being.

Think of something in nature that you can identify with—maybe you feel as sturdy as a tree, as quick as a cheetah, as still as a mountain. Then use Van Sertima's form to write about how you are like that object. First, introduce the object of comparison by saying how you aren't like it: "I have no leaves to give to the wind, my arms aren't dark with thick strong bark . . ." and then assert how you are: "but I am a tree, wildly waving, loving the sky, absorbing the sun for food, loving the dirt in my feet . . .".

163

Can you remember a time when you were younger and felt scared? What color does that memory make you think of? What object is that the color of? Write a poem about the memory in which you use or talk about the color.

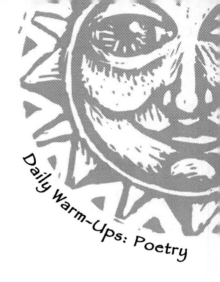

164

Write a poem revealing a secret you kept when you were younger that doesn't seem so important now. See if you can remember when you stopped caring or thinking about it. You might want to start: "I never would have told anyone . . ." and describe the secret and why you felt you had to keep it. Then write about what has changed since then.

165

An **oxymoron** is a descriptive phrase that contains words with opposite meanings. For example, "jumbo shrimp" is an oxymoron because a shrimp is very small and often means something very small. Other oxymorons might be "bright night," or "heavy air," or "small world." Can you think of another oxymoron? Write a poem about your oxymoron in which you explain how it is true. For instance, a poem about a jumbo shrimp might talk about how big the jumbo shrimp are compared to all the smaller ones and other tiny sea creatures.

166

Look through the pictures in a book or a bunch of photographs and find a picture of someone you find interesting. Imagine walking into the picture to interview the person. Ask questions about what he or she is doing in the scene and what he or she is thinking about; also ask personal questions about the person's history and family. Invent the answers and then write a poem about the person. You may want to describe the scene of the picture.

William Wordsworth wrote a poem, "To Toussaint L'Ouverture, Leader of the African Slaves of San Domingo, Imprisoned by Napoleon," to a man whose strength and leadership he admired. When Wordsworth wrote the poem, Toussaint L'Ouverture was in jail.

O miserable Chieftain! where and when
   Wilt thou find patience! Yet die not; do thou
   Wear rather in thy bonds a cheerful brow:
Though fallen thyself, never to rise again,
Live, and take comfort. Thou hast left behind
   Powers that will work for thee; air, earth, and skies;
There's not a breathing of the common wind
   That will forget thee; thou hast great allies;
   Thy friends are exultations, agonies,
And love, and man's unconquerable mind.

168

Write a poem to someone you admire. It may be someone who has been discouraged, like Toussaint. You might want to choose a political leader (the person can be historical). Be creative as you explain why the person is great; you can use natural imagery, in the way that Wordsworth says the "air, earth, and skies" will never forget Toussaint.

Daily Warm-Ups: Poetry

Daily Warm-Ups: Poetry

Write a very long sentence that you like the sound of. Then make it into two different poems, one with three lines and one with six. Which poem sounds better? Which works better with the idea of the sentence? Choose the one you like best and revise it a little, to make it really good.

169

Have you ever kept a journal or diary? In the late 1950s, some poets began writing poetry about their secret feelings or private lives. They included personal details as if they were writing in a journal, and the poetry came to be called confessional. Many poets today write confessional poetry.

Write a confessional poem. You don't have to disclose any big secrets, but you should write openly and with the feeling that the poem is like a journal entry. You can write about something that happened yesterday that you haven't told anyone about. Include personal feelings and details from your specific experience as much as possible.

170

Write a four-line poem that has to do with quiet, still things. Then write a four-line poem that has lots of noise and action. Now, try to make those two poems into one. You can alternate lines, or words, or put one on top of the other, whatever, as long as you have one combined eight-line poem in the end. What is your new long poem about? Give it a title.

Helen Hunt Jackson's poem "Friends" describes a meeting of friends who haven't seen each other in a year:

> We rode a day, from east, from west,
> To meet. A year had done its best,
> By absence, and by loss of speech,
> To put beyond the other's reach
> Each heart and life; but, drawing nigh,
> 'Ah! It is you!' 'Yes, it is I!'

Write a poem in which you describe seeing someone you haven't seen in a long time. You may want to start with the journey each of you takes to meet, as Jackson does. Try to write about the details of the meeting, and your mixed emotions as it happens—you might feel nervous, excited, scared, or happy, all of these at the same time.

172

Think of an experience that didn't go well for you. Maybe you tried to glue something heavy onto your wall, or make a cake without a recipe, or play tennis without an opponent, or have a party with your dog. Imagine that a friend or sibling is about to try the same thing. Write a poem of advice on what not to do. Feel free to exaggerate. For example:

> How to bake a cake:
> Don't put in the eggshells
> Don't try to take the sugar out with your fingers when
>   you put too much in
> Don't crush a candy bar with a potato masher and try to
>   use it for icing…

173

In ancient Greek and Roman mythology, a muse was a goddess who inspired poets. Some poems therefore begin with an "invocation to the muse," in which the poet asks the muse for her help and inspiration. In this poem by Anne Killigrew, the poet describes her request to the muse:

> O queen of verse, said I, if thou'lt inspire,
> And warm my soul with thy poetic fire
> No love of gold shall share with thee my heart,
> Or yet ambition in my breast have part,
> More rich, more noble I will ever hold
> The Muse's laurel, than a crown of gold.

174

The invocation to the muse can also be more specific, asking the muse for her help in telling a specific story. Write the beginning of a poem in which you ask a muse for inspiration or for help writing a poem about a certain subject.

Daily Warm-Ups: Poetry

Ralph Waldo Emerson ends his poem "Each and All" by describing a scene in which he realizes something important:

> . . . As I spoke, beneath my feet
> The ground-pine curled its pretty wreath,
> Running over the club-moss burrs;
> I inhaled the violet's breath;
> Around me stood the oaks and firs;
> Pine-cones and acorns lay on the ground;
> Over me soared the eternal sky,
> Full of light and of deity;
> Again I saw, again I heard,
> The rolling river, the morning bird;—
> Beauty through my senses stole;
> I yielded myself to the perfect whole.

Emerson is overcome by the beauty around him and finally sees it as a "perfect whole." Can you remember a time when you realized something, and felt that you suddenly knew something important and real? Write a poem in which you are realizing something important. Like Emerson, write about the details of the moment when you finally grasped it.

175

© 2003 J. Weston Walch, Publisher

An epigram is a very short poem, usually two lines, that says something interesting or witty. Here is an epigram called "Dreams" by Robert Herrick ("several" is used to mean "separate"):

> Here we are all, by day; by night, we're hurled
> By dreams, each one into a several world.

Write an epigram about dreams, or some other aspect of night—stars, the moon, darkness, or sleeping. You'll want to say something general, but insightful, about your topic.

Daily Warm-Ups: Poetry

176

Anne Bradstreet lived in Colonial America and wrote a poem called "To My Dear Children." Write a letter poem to yourself in the voice of a parent or grandparent. You may want to imagine your parents' voices and the kinds of things they say and then write it down as a poem. Try to make the poem really sound as if it is coming from an adult.

Daily Warm-Ups: Poetry

177

Write an imperative poem telling someone how to build or make something. It can be something you really know about or something you're guessing at. You may want to start off with the materials or tools needed and then narrate as if you're watching the person put the thing together.

178

Write five lines that you could imagine using as endings to poems.

© 2003 J. Weston Walch, Publisher

What makes a poem a poem? Write your answer as a poem.

180

Turn downtime into learning time!

Other books in the

Daily *Warm-Ups* series:

- Algebra
- Analogies
- Biology
- Critical Thinking
- Earth Science
- Geography
- Geometry
- Journal Writing

- Pre-Algebra
- Shakespeare
- Spelling & Grammar
- Test-Prep Words
- U.S. History
- Vocabulary
- Writing
- World History